The Fruits of Christ

The Fruits of Christ
Tommy R. Morris

Copyright © 2009 by Tommy R. Morris

All rights reserved. No part of this book may be reproduced, stored, or transmitted by any means—whether auditory, graphic, mechanical, or electronic—without written permission of both publisher and author, except in the case of brief excerpts used in critical articles and reviews. Unauthorized reproduction of any part of this work is illegal and is punishable by law.

ISBN: 978-0-578-01419-7

PREFACE

I am a blessed person, because of God's love for me, which has always been there. Mine has not always been a life of joy; I have had my share of difficulties. Nevertheless, the love of the Lord has picked me up, has carried me, and has raised me to new heights in Christ Jesus.

My mother brought us up in the church, but we still did not know anything about accepting Christ into our hearts. This is where I thought the church in those days, lacked the inspiration it needed, to be able to lead a person into a personal relationship with Christ.

My brother Ronald, my best friend Jessie McHenry, and I always followed God. However, since those days, we have had many experiences, and supernatural things of God manifested in our lives. Moreover, what I have learned about my journey in this walk with Christ, I would like to tell you about it in this little book, which the Lord has put on my heart to write. The titles that I use are the "light bulb" moments that came on, at different times in my life, through sermons, circumstances, situations, and relationships. Altogether, they paint a picture of a glorious Lord.

I believe you will find this book easy to read, and easy to understand. Therefore, as I invite you to listen to the story of my journey with Christ, I would like to ask a question on truth. Will we who trust in God and seek Him find help and protection? "God is the help of those who seek Him." Listen to the words of the Psalmist who wrote:

> "I will lift up my eyes to the hills, from whence comes my help? My help *comes* from the Lord, who made heaven and earth. He will not allow your foot to be moved; He who keeps you will not

slumber. Behold, He who keep Israel, shall neither slumber, nor sleep. The Lord *is* your keeper; the Lord *is* your shade at your right hand. The sun shall not strike you by day, Nor the moon by night. The Lord shall preserve you from all evil; He shall preserve your soul. The Lord shall preserve your going out and you're coming in, From this time forth, and even forevermore (Ps. 121: 1-8 NKJV)."

According to Acts 17:28 NKJV, "for in Him we live and move and have our being." Furthermore, Phil 1:11 NKJV says, "Being filled with the fruits of righteousness which are by Jesus Christ, to the glory and praise of God," in my opinion refers to us as the fruits of Christ who are also His offspring. Therefore, God is very responsible for our lives, as a fruit tree is for the fruit it bears. As long as we will connect to the vine, we will reflect that to which we are connected. This is why it is so important that we accept Christ as our partner in life, because as His partner, we receive the benefits of that partnership, and of that connection. Like life-giving sap, flowing through a tree which carries food and water to all its parts. I pray that this book will aid you in your desire for a better connection to the source, which is Christ. My prayer is that, as a result of reading this book, you will bear more fruit and develop a more intimate relationship with our Savior.[1]

---

[1](All Scripture quotations are taken from the Nelson Study Bible, New King James Version, Thomas Nelson Publishers, Nashville).

CONTENTS

Chapter 1	The Fruit's of Christ!	1
Chapter 2	He Raised Me	13
Chapter 3	He Carried Me	21
Chapter 4	There is Protected Ground Inside of You!	27
Chapter 5	The Lord, The Defender of his People	33
Chapter 6	We Have to be Sincere!	39
Chapter 7	The Substance Is Of Christ	43
Chapter 8	The Holy Spirit Will Take Me Where He Has Ordained Me	49
Chapter 9	Absolute Trust	55
Chapter 10	The Seed Is The Doorstop That Props Open The Door.	59
Chapter 11	Sailing in a Stormy Season	65
Chapter 12	Hidden in the Lord	69

CHAPTER 1

The Fruit's of Christ!

"I am the true vine, and My Father is the vinedresser. Every branch in me that does not bear fruit He takes away; and every branch that bears fruit He prunes, that it may bear more fruit. You are already clean because of the word, which I have spoken to you. Abide in Me, and I in you. As the branch cannot bear fruit of itself, unless it abides in the vine, neither can you, unless you abide in me." I am the vine, you are the branches. He who abides in me, and I in him, bears much fruit; for without me you can do nothing. If no one abides in Me, he is cast out as a branch and is withered; and they gather them and throw them into the fire, and they are burned. If you abide in Me, and my words abide in you, you will ask what you desire, and it shall be done for you. By this My Father is glorified, that you bear much fruit; so you shall be My disciples (John 15: 1-8)."

The life-giving sap, the juice that flows through a tree carrying food, and water is the like nature of God in us, because He is responsible for our being. If we have this life-giving sap, then the fruits of Christ would be so evident in our lives that there would be no doubt, to whom we belong. That is why learning the art of love will always give us a reputation, that boasts of Jesus Christ's life in our lives, which benefits and enlightens morally and spiritually. Christ will transport us from one place to another, bearing the responsibility of keeping and making ourselves available to love. Moreover, Christ will manifest His love in our lives. Faith enables us to come to God, but love enables us to imitate him. Therefore, we are the fruits of Christ incarnated.

God is love, so God in his infinite love has lifted us and has raised us from an unfavorable place in our lives, to a higher place to bring glory to His name. (Moreover, if we live in love, and live in God, God is in us.) When we live in love, then we will be unashamed when Jesus returns. Therefore, to elevate our spirit, God has designed love to pick us up, to raise us up, and to carry us to new heights in Christ Jesus. The greatest gift that God has given to us is love: if we do not live in love, it profits us nothing (1 Cor 13: 1-13).

Therefore, (1 John 4:11 NKJV) says, "Beloved, if God so loved us, we also ought to love one another." We feel pain and distress from beginning to end. Moreover, we have a readiness to please others, and a good-natured disposition. When we direct our love toward others, we rejoice in the blessings they receive, rather than desiring those blessings for ourselves. The selfless love of God, to which God calls us, does not involve pride or glory. True love does not seek its own, and if we truly love others, we would set aside our own plans, and agendas, and entitlements for the good of another.

Furthermore, if we live in love, we will not disrespect others and we will not be impolite or cause people to be angry. We will not be overly sensitive, either. If we truly love others, we would be careful not to be touchy, concerning other people's words, or actions toward us. Godly love has nothing to do with evil, but has everything to do with what is right and true.

Love does not mean that we are blind or naïve. When we love, we may recognize problems, and failures in people, but we do not lose faith in the possibilities of what people might become. Love never gives up, knowing that God can change lives for the better. Love accepts any hardship, or rejection, but continues unabated to build up, and encourage. Love determines what is best for another person, and then does it. God planted this love in our spirit to pick us up, to raise us, and to carry us to the place He has purposed for us. It is a giving, selfless, expect-nothing-in-return kind of love. True love puts up with people who would be easier to give up on. You may be gifted with many gifts, but they become useless without love.

He Picked Me Up

> "Love suffers long and is kind; love does not envy; love does not parade itself, is not puffed up; does not behave rudely, does not seek its own, is not provoked, thinks no evil; does not rejoice in iniquity, but rejoices in the truth; bears all things, believes all things, hopes all things, endures all things. Love never fails (1 Cor 13: 4-8a NKJV)."

My journey begins, when I graduated from high school. I joined the army and enlisted for four years. I was a wire systems installer and switchboard operator. During that time, I got into a lot of things that I was not used to doing. I grew up in the church but I had not known Jesus Christ as my personal Savior. I had a great sense of God's hand on my life, and I knew that God was watching over me. Moreover, I always talked with God during my time in the military, because you were always in dangerous, life-threatening situations.

I talked with the Father often, and I was always singing spiritual songs in the shower. One of the songs that I was singing was, *"When I get to Heaven"*, and the guy's would always tell me that, I made them home sick. They enjoyed the song, and they would always tell me how they felt the presence of God. I made many friends, and I shared moral and spiritual advice with them. I say all of this because I believe that God picked me up, even though I did not know him as my Lord. He was with me throughout my time in the service.

In 1980, a friend of my brother and I, were at his house, smoking marijuana, and listening to Christian radio. My brother, who at the time was confessing to be an atheist, was sitting on the floor by the radio, when all of a sudden he started shaking and began foaming at the mouth. Jessie and I were paralyzed, asking one another, whether we should call 911, but we decided to wait a minute. Just as we were about to call for help, he stopped and said,

"Why didn't we tell him?" over and over again.

We then said to him, "Tell you what?"

He said, "Jesus is real,"

I said, "That's what we have been trying to tell you."

Then I asked him what had happened to him. He said that as he was listening to the radio, the speaker said something that he had agreed with, and all of a sudden, he was moving at the speed of light. He then came to a door, then he heard a voice that said "The door is closing and no man can open it," so he jumped up and stuck his hands between the door and started trying to squeeze his body through the other side, and he squeezed himself through to the other side and fell through. He came to himself and said, "Why didn't we tell him?"

What I believe happened at that time, was that he heard the speaker say a truth, and he then believed that truth. I was shocked that he would accept truth, since he was an atheist; it was not common for him to except truth. Therefore, at the time, he said within himself, *I believe that truth*, the Holy Spirit moved in and changed his life forever. I am talking about how God picks us up, and takes us to higher places in Christ Jesus. Even when we have not asked to be saved, He helps us. After that wonderful experience, we continued reading the word of God and he led us to, Isaiah 29:9 NKJV: "Pause and wonder! Blind yourselves and be blind! They are drunk, but not with wine; They stagger, but not with intoxicating drink."

We were exactly the way the scripture said we were, and our loving Father never stopped loving us in spite of our condition. This night was the night that our lives were change forever; we all had accepted Jesus as our personal savior. In addition, God the father called all three of us into the ministry; we all accepted Him at different times. This was the start of many, difficulties, in each of our ministries. We started a bible study group, and called it the, "Fruit's of Christ Ministry," we were on television, on the radio, and started a Christian singing group called, "Sabbath." We were ministering in our home state of Texas and in Louisiana.

However, it was at that point that the enemy started his attacks on each of us in our walks with the Lord. Although we had knowledge of God, we did not know God, because we were immature in the gospel. This is where we began to grow apart. Moreover, our marriages were ending, it was an, all-out assault on our families. We never denied our faith, but we turned our backs on the local body of believers/congregation, which we thought had failed us. We fell into sin, we all went different ways, and did not speak for years.

God, started picking us up again, drawing us back one by one, and loving us. In John 15:1-8 NKJV, God began to reveal to me how much I was apart from the true vine, as well as from His church that has been fruitless as His reflection on the earth. In addition, He showed me how I and the church had missed His love for me and the church. When I came back to the church, I did not see it the same way as I had before. I did not criticize, judge, disapprove, or find fault with the church, because I was not the vine, I was a branch.

Christ Brings Division

In this journey with Christ, I have experienced division on every level, from family members, denominations, friends and foes alike. In addition to our relationship with Christ, we were put out of churches, and rejected by family, we lost friends with whom we had grown up with, and we made enemies with people we had worked with for years (Luke 12: 49-53 NKJV).

Jesus emphasized that a disciple must have clear priorities. The call of God should receive priority over everything else. Leave all to follow Christ; he offers peace to those who respond to him. A decision for Jesus could mean rejection by family and persecution, even to the point of death. Those who are fearful of their family's disapproval or persecution will not come to Jesus, because they could possibly lose their family. Jesus is calling us to follow him in the way of rejection and suffering. Moreover, He is urging the people to think about what it would mean to follow him, and not to take it lightly.

It has often been those closest to us who have rejected us, and our message, even to the point of betrayal. Those who refuse that kind of discipleship will experience great loss. Taking up the cross here stands for commitment to the extent of being willing to die for something. God commanded us to remember Christ's resurrection. Being raised from the dead emphasizes that our Savior lives today and is seated at the right hand of God the father.

Human circumstances cannot confine the word of God, whether through a tract, a book, a bible, or a simple statement. God uses his word to accomplish His purposes (Isaiah 55.11). There are numerous examples of people who were antagonistic to God's truth, but who eventually surrendered their lives to God when he kept after them. We must not hide the gospel, but instead let it go forth unchained in spite of our on limitations.

We have unity with Christ in his death and resurrection through baptism, which becomes our death to sin, and our resurrection to eternal life (Romans 6). Persevering in the faith even in the face of hardship, or persecution will result in a reward when Christ returns. If believers deny the endurance of persecution for Christ, he will deny them the reward, and the reign that could have been theirs. *Faithless* describes the life of an, "immature believer," who lives for himself, and not for the savior. Even when believers fail the Savior, he remains loyal. For Christ to abandon us would be contrary to his faithful nature.[2]

Breaking the Chain

Breaking the chain is like breaking a covenant, or breaking an agreement; it is also like breaking a relationship, or breaking a friendship. The Bible here teaches me the importance of keeping the agreement that I have made with my Savior, no matter what comes my way.

We must maintain our covenant with God, and the only way to maintain our covenant with God is by faith.

> "These are grumblers, complainers, walking according to their own lusts; and they mouth great swelling words, flattering people to gain advantage. But you, beloved, remember the words, which were spoken before by the apostles of our Lord Jesus Christ: how they told you that there would be markers in the last time who would walk according to their own ungodly lusts. These are sensual persons, who cause divisions, not having the spirit (Jude 16-19 NKJV)".

---

[2](See Matthew 10: 34-39; Luke 9:57-62 ;12:49-53; 14:25-33 ; 2 Timothy 2:8-26 ; 2 Timothy 3:1-17 NKJV, Thomas Nelson Publishers, Nashville)

This is where the the churches that we fellowshipped with came to disagree and began persecuting us. Those traditions were taking away from God's word in the life of new coverts. Therefore, we became alienated because of our uncompromising commitment to the word of God. However, the person who knows God shall be strong, and refuse to break the chain for traditional loyalties.

Christians who understood God's word, allowed to go through troubled times so that they could be refined, and purified. A remnant of followers broke away from the church and joined our ministry, expressed its faith in what God has said; therefore, they understood the fact that Christ suffered in our place.

"And those of the people who understand shall instruct many; yet for many days they shall fall by sword and flame, by captivity and plundering. Now when they fall, they shall be aided with a little help; but many shall join with them by intrigue. And some of those of understanding shall fall, to refine them, purify them, and make them white, until the time of the end; because it is still for the appointed time (Dan 11:33-35 NKJV)."

Satan will succeed until the time of wrath is complete, for what has been determined will surely take place; Satan will honor those who submit to him,

"And shall cause them to rule over many, and divide the land for gain (Dan 11:39 NKJV)."

His time will suddenly run out, and there will be no one to help him. Peace is what sums up Christ's ministry of reconciliation, justification, adoption, and glorification. When we as His people are at peace or rest we are at the place where we are used of the Father. Everyone who is crucified with Christ is dying to sin, the law, and "this present evil age." While believers live on physically, Christ also lives within them spiritually. Christ's resurrection power through the spirit is at work through the Christian, who chooses to live by faith in the Son of God.

"I have been crucified with Christ; it is no longer I who live, but Christ lives in me; and the life which I now live in the flesh I live by faith in the son of God, who loved me and gave himself for me. I do not set aside the grace of God; for if righteousness comes through the law, then Christ died in vain (Gal 2:20 NKJV)."

Therefore, I live my life in this earthly body by trusting in the Son of God, who loved me, and gave himself for me. I am not one of those who treat the grace of God as meaningless. By faith we overcome, and are made perfect, "made complete." This completion, the realization of God's promises with Christ coming kingdom, awaits all believers. Therefore, we should not be afraid of the enemy, and break the chain that we have made with our lord, and Savior, Jesus Christ.[3]

It's A Matter of the Heart

True worship is a matter of the heart; true worship is reflecting his ways in your life every day.

True worship indicates a strong belief and deep conviction; this is a wonderful example of a sufferer passionately expressing his determination to cling to his faith even in the middle of a horrible situation. These verses contrast human limitations with the sovereignty of God.

Man can plan, dream, and hope, but the outcome is from the lord. Rather than "resign ourselves to fate," we should trust in God. Our loving Father is in control of our seemingly chaotic situations.

Elaborating on this theme, in addition to being sovereign, God is the final judge. All the injustices in this world will be corrected some glorious day. The word "commit" (Prov 16:3 NKJV) is from a word meaning, "to roll," so the idea is to "roll your cares on to the Lord." Trusting the Lord with your decisions frees you from preoccupation with your problems.

---

[3](See Isaiah 53:5; Daniel 11: 29-32 ; Hebrews 11:37-38 NKJV)

The proud in heart are warned as well: pride has everything backwards. It takes credit away from the giver, who gives graciously, and awards it to the receiver, who takes without thanking. That is why God sees it, as an abomination. The word *abomination* throughout the book of Proverbs, refers to God's disgust.

Mercy and truth are translated by a *'genuine reverence,"* *reconciliation* probably indirectly, refers to a "sacrificial offering," but not apart from a contrite heart. here is respect for God, and turns a person away from evil. The book of Proverbs often speaks of wealth as the reward of wisdom and virtue, but not always; righteousness is the real treasure.

A *highway* is a thoroughfare, a metaphor for the way a person lives consistently. An upright person's "highway," or lifestyle, is to depart from evil; he does not compromise, and he consistently strives to do well. Wisdom is never easily gained or quickly achieved, that is why a wise person increases learning. Those who possess understanding have access to a fountain of life that constantly renews itself, and is available to everyone. The phrase *wellspring of life* is an image of salvation; water was essential for life in the dry regions of ancient Israel.

The wise know they are ignorant, so they keep on learning. The condition for righteousness, which comes from being justified, is one's internal faith. Salvation means deliverance from wrath, and from the power of sin. Salvation also results from an external confession, which is calling on the Lord for help (Rom 10:10). We are sure of the presence of eternal life within us, when we demonstrate self-sacrificial love to others. Believers, who have been truly loved, will know their behavior has its source in the truth, and therefore, will have confidence before God. Love benefits the giver and the receiver both.

Our hearts condemns us, in that we recognize that we do not measure up to the standard of love, and we feel insecure in approaching God. Our conscience may not acknowledge the loving deeds we have done in the power of the Holy Spirit, but God does, and he is superior to our hearts. Unlike our conscience,

God considers everything, including Christ's atoning work for us. God is more compassionate, and understanding toward us than we sometimes are toward ourselves.

As a person thinks in his heart, so is he; how do thoughts get into the heart, the seat of reflection? Through the eyes, ears, and other senses, we take into our mind the raw materials of the experiences and actions around us, and allow them to settle in our hearts. David put it this way: "your words have I hidden in my heart that I might not sin against you" (Ps 119:11 NKJV). The other side of this is, "I will set nothing wicked before my eyes" (Ps 101:3 NKJV). Paul pictured the believer as "bringing every thought into captivity to the obedience of Christ" (2Cor 10:5).

Simon, who was a new believer, thought that he could receive God's miracles by paying for them. He confused the work of God with his previous magical practices, because others had paid him for the secrets of his magic. He may have thought that, this was the best way to approach Peter, but he soon learned the error of his ways. The character of the new man is not to serve or perform a function as expected in the body of Christ, but to be equally included in all the groups in God's family.

"Let the word of Christ dwell in you richly" *(Col 3:16)* is apparently a parallel thought to Paul's statement where he says, "Be filled with the spirit" (Eph 5:18). Both and in Ephesians 5, the result of being, "filled," with the Spirit or the Word of Christ is singing. Paul sums up how Christians should live, and we should commit everything we do, and say to Jesus, and continually thank God for all his good gifts.[4]

---

[4](See Proverbs 16:1-9, 17-18, 20-23, 19-21; Matthew 15:18-19; Mark 7:6-8; Acts 8:21-22; Romans 10:10; Colossians 3:12-17; 1John 3:19-21 NKJV.)

CHAPTER 2

He Raised Me

I focus my belief upon the God of resurrection power, who motivated me to face difficulties, danger, and death for Christ's sake. I rested in what I knew about God, not in how I felt. All of the suffering that I endured brought good to others and glory to God. I have concluded that we should not lose heart, because God will raise us up with Jesus.

Here is a great principle: a proper focus on our glorious future with Christ will empower us to endure any kind of trouble. Afflictions produce glory, but the glory balances out the affliction and brings harmony to one's life. Trials are light, and temporary compared to the eternal glory we will receive. focusing on the future, enabled me to properly assess problems and see how small they were compared to their eternal results. In order not to lose heart, the believer needs to shift his or her focus from that which seen to that which is not seen, from the temporary problems to the glorious eternal rewards he or she will receive.

The ability to survive and succeed, totally rests upon our dependence, on our Father. God raised up the Lord Jesus and He will raise us up by His power. We can know that He who raised the Lord Jesus will also raise, us up with Him and will present us with Him (2 Cor 4:14). We must rest in what we know about God, not how we feel. God will raise us to the level in life where we should be, if we trust in Him and totally depend on Him for everything. There nothing He will not do for us if we would completely rely on Him and believe in Him.

When we are weak, He is strong, and that is exactly how God like's it.

Jesus said, "I am the bread of life. He who comes to Me shall never hunger, and he who believes in Me shall never thirst" (John 6:35).

Cry to the Father and He will raise you, just as He raised me. What I like about a personal relationship with Christ the call is, to confess your sins, to repent, and to believe on the Lord Jesus Christ. This is great! You cannot ask for anything any better than this, and the finished work is up to the Holy Spirit.[5]

Consider Your Ways

As Christians, we are asked to think about whether our habits, activities, and attitudes demonstrate good judgment before the Lord. God asked us to take stock of our lives. Although we eat, and drink, we never seem satisfied. Although we put on clothes, we never feel warm. Although we earn wages, we constantly feel as though our pockets have holes in them through which our money is lost.

Christian's must be in harmony with the sacrifices we make: "You did not turn to me," God said. Despite God withholding his blessings, we have not fully turned back to him. To this day, God is determined to bring his blessings on his people, but he demands us to recognize him as the source of our great productivity. Some are blinded, because we do not believe, and we are spiritually uninterested. This is a continual pattern, as

---

[5](1Corinthians 6:14 ; 2 Corinthians 4:14; James 5:15 NKJV)

it would be through our continual rejection of Christ, which would bring upon us untold misery as a nation.

The word division means, *"to stand apart,"* or *"to cause dissension."* Strife and rivalry cause dissension, which eventually leads to divisions in a church. Such dissension causes an offense that becomes a snare or obstacle to others. Contentious and divisive people, who will cause others to stumble, should be avoided. Divisive people destroy the peace, and the unity of a church, but God, who is the source of peace, will crush this work of Satan through the wisdom, and the obedience of believers. Ultimately, God will totally defeat Satan, and bring peace to the whole church.

Paul pleaded for an outward expression that came from an inward spirit. Not only did Paul encourage the Corinthians to speak the same thing, and to have external unity, but he also urged them to be joined together in a unity of hearts and minds. Christian life not only is compared here to running or standing still, but to a walk that is worthy: A believer's life should match the excellence of Christ's calling, and long with his lowliness, gentleness, and longsuffering. These are the attitudes that Jesus demonstrated when he was on earth. These attitudes do not come naturally; you must cultivate them by your determination to place others above yourself. Only the spirit can empower us to treat people this way consistently. The word *bearing* is very close to our expression, "putting up with (Gal 6:2 NKJV)." It describes being patient with the shortcomings of others. Often we ask God to be patient with our own failings, and yet do not exercise the same type of patience ourselves. *Unity of the Spirit*: expresses that all Christians are one in the Spirit; it is our duty to keep, or observe that unity, recognize it as real, and act upon it without a narrow-minded spirit. *Endeavoring* means, to make every effort, to work hard at maintaining the unity of the spirit.[6]

---

[6](Haggai 1:5, 7, 12-14; Romans 16:17-20;1Corinthians 1:10; Ephesians 4:1-6 NKJV)

What Would You Have Me Do Lord?

"What would you have me do Lord?" "I would have you saved and to do yourself no harm, and to believe on the Lord Jesus Christ." He would have me to be faithful, and not harden my heart. Whoever believes in Him is not condemned; but he who does not believe is condemned already (Jn 3:18 NKJV). This is what He would have me do so I could live. If I show mercy and have compassion, He would have me to show mercy to my neighbors.

However, do not forget to do well and to share with joy, but not with grief, for that would be unprofitable for you. He will complete you to do his will, so let us continually offer the sacrifice of praise to God, which is the fruit of our lips, giving thanks to His name. People neither understand spiritual truth nor do they diligently seek after God. People are satisfied with externals, with being "religious." God's standard of living is through trust, there by excluding boasting, and He only wants us to boast in Him. It is for God's glory and for the best for others.

Give no offense, but encourage fellow Christians, to spread the good news about Christ. Even if it means restricting your freedom, do not seek your own way, or anything else for your own pleasure; instead, desire to help others. True ability, as much as is needed or desired, is found in the strength of Christ.

The character of the new man is that he should commit everything he does or says to Jesus and continually thank God, for all of His good gifts. Respond to God in awe, reverence, and wonder, serve God in purity of action, and to avoid evil, and do not worship of any material thing in God's universe.

He will equip us with all we need to do His will. We can do nothing apart from Christ, and a believer cannot accomplish anything of permanent spiritual value without Christ. Beware of self-confidence or trusting in oneself. The problem here is not our plans, nor the concept of planning; it is leaving God out of our plans.[7]

Only Believe

As soon as Jesus heard the word that was spoken, "He said to the ruler of the synagogue, "Do not be afraid; only believe (Mark 5:36 NKJV)."

Because of the death report, that came from the ruler of the synagogue he assumed her condition was now irreversible, and that there was not a remedy. Jesus immediately corrected his thoughts by insisting that Jairus stop being afraid and continue believing in Him. Jairus believed God for his daughter's healing, but as soon as the report came that she was dead, he began to regret, that he had failed to get to Jesus on time. This fear led to doubt. Jesus, knowing all the emotions that, Jairus was experiencing, responded by correcting his thoughts.

We as Christ followers must imitate him, in everything we do. Jesus listened to the people that came from Jairus house to tell him that his daughter was dead. We too must have our ears open to hear, the things that are being said around us, so that we can speak to the spirit of doubt, and fear, that comes to make people afraid. We should respond immediately, as Jesus responded with Jairus, because the quicker we respond, the better chance we have in stopping the seed of doubt and fear.

The enemy comes to steal, kill, and destroy the faith of God's children. As Jesus' compassion for Jairus, caused him to respond immediately, so shall our response be, to attack immediately the words that come from the enemy. We should

---

[7](See Acts 16:30-31; John 3:17-18;15:5,19; Hebrews 3: 7-19; Luke 10:28, 37; Hebrews 13:15-21; Romans 3:11;1 Corinthians 10:30-33; Philippians 4:13; Colossians 3:17; James 4:13-17 NKJV.)

have love, and sympathy for our brothers and sisters, just as Christ has. When we reprove and rebuke by sharing the truth we are helping our brothers and sisters to defeat the wiles of the enemy. Come what may we must continue to trust, believe, depend, and have confidence in Christ. No matter what the situation, circumstances, troubles, and problems, having faith in God is essential. There can be no greater expression of the love of God, then for him to want us to trust in him, to cast all of our burdens on him, to protect us, and to provide for us.

Jesus wants us to have one purpose alone, without anyone or anything else. Believe.

He's My Friend

We are still friend, "No matter what comes my way, I will still trust you with my life, and stay connected to You. I have been through rejection, lied on, unemployed, broke, and shamed. However, I still experience complete confidence, and security, because you are my family, and I have a legal position because of your grace. It is because of a deep abiding fellowship, which is why Jesus moved us from servants to friends.

This involved a process of discipline concerning his commandments. No plant produces fruit instantaneously; fruit is the result of a process. Such is also the case with believers. All of our situations, circumstances, troubles, and problems, have everything to do with lifting us up to promote better growth. Once the fruit is on the vine, the vinedresser cleanses the fruit of bugs and diseases. The spiritual counterpart is cleansing, done through the word. For the branch to produce more fruit, it must abide, which means to dwell, to stay, to settle in, and to sink deeper. The way to abide in Christ is to obey, and the believer who lovingly obeys the word of God produces much fruit.

Apart from Christ, a believer cannot accomplish anything of permanent spiritual value. Not abiding in Christ has serious consequences, including the loss of fellowship, a loss of vitality, and a loss of rewards. Failure to abide produces spiritual disaster. Where there is good fruit there are seeds to reproduce. The Father's love for the Son is the measure of the Son's love for believers. Christ loves believers unconditionally, but as believers obey Christ's words and abide in his love, they come to experience and understand his love for them more and more. When we experience Christ's love, there is complete joy.

To abide, a believer must obey. To obey, a believer must love other believers. Jesus is our model for love: Intimacy with Him is the motive for loving as He loves. If believers obey His command to love, they enjoy the intimacy of His friendship. Friendship, unlike son ship, is not a once-for-all gift, but develops as the result of obeying Jesus' command to love.

A servant does what he is told, and sees that, which his master does, but does not necessarily know the meaning or purpose of it. A friend knows what is happening because friends develop deep fellowship by communicating with one another. Jesus had initiated the relationship with His disciples. It started with selection, moved to servant ood, and grew to friendship. Having chosen the disciples, Jesus commissioned them to bring forth permanent fruit through prayer.[8]

---

[9](See also Is 46:3-5; John 15:1-16 ; Acts 17:28; Matthew 11: 28 -30; Jn 21:18; Is 56:3,6 NKJV)

CHAPTER 3

He Carried Me

In the Spirit describes a spiritually exalted state; it is as if He sweeps us away. In addition, it indicates the Lord is never ceasing care for His children, even when they become old. God said,

> "I created you and have cared for you since before you were born". I will be your God throughout your lifetime, until your hair is white with age. I made you, and I will care for you, I will carry you along and save you" (Is 46:3-5 NKJV).

There are activities that God perform on behalf of His children, that only He can do for them. When we were younger we walked where we wished, moved about without restriction. Nevertheless, when we became older, we had to stretch out our hands, looking for help. The day will come when we will totally be under the control of someone else, carrying us where we would not wish to go (Jn 21:18).

No matter what situations, problems, or troubles we face, our God is always there. Though there will always be storms, he will never leave us, and will always carry us. Though we may be in a storm and feel as though God has left us alone, the reality is that He has not left us, but He is carrying us.

We can do nothing without God, though He is not far from each one of us. "In Him we live, and move, and have our being" (Acts 17:28). God is upholding us, which means he is "bearing" or "carrying," us, and this refers to movement and progress toward an end. In Matthew 11: 28 -30, the Lord say's, "Come to me, all you who labor and are heavy laden, and I will give you rest. Take my yoke upon you and learn from me, for I am gentle and lowly in heart, and you will find rest for your souls. For My yoke is easy, and my burden is light." Our Father desires to carry and bear us up. Father please carry us![9]

Joined at the Heart

We will be given absolute assurance by the all-powerful and all-knowing God that those who are joined at the heart with Him will not be lost. Isaiah prophesied of foreigners who would convert to the worship of the true Lord. These foreigners would demonstrate saving faith and thereby would be counted among those converted. God's blessings are for everyone who commits himself or herself to the Lord.

The Lord revealed to me, "Do not let them think that I consider them as second-class citizens: They are as much mine as anyone else's, when they choose to do what pleases me and commit their lives to me." God will bless those who commit themselves to the Him, and serve him with their whole hearts, love his name, and do not desecrate the day of rest.

In addition, He will fill those who have accepted His covenant with joy in His house of prayer. He reaches down to lift up those who will humble themselves before Him. He is able to give all of his time to each of His children; He is not bound by the succession of moments that limits our experience. No one seems to understand that God is protecting him or her from evil to come.

God lives in that high and holy place with those whose spirits are contrite and humble. God refreshes the humble and gives new courage to those with repentant hearts. God sees what we do, but still heals us anyway.

> "I will lead them and comfort those who mourn. Then words of praise will be on their lips, and may they have peace, for I will heal them all (ref. Is. 61: 2, 3 NKJV)".

We can gather our thoughts, but the Lord gives the right answer.

Commit your works unto the Lord, and your plans will succeed. When the ways of the people please the Lord, he makes even their enemies live at peace with them. We can make our plans, but the Lord determines our steps. The path of the upright leads away from evil; whosoever follows that path is safe. Those who listen to instruction will prosper; those who trust the Lord will be happy. Wise people are known for their understanding and they appreciate instruction, if it is well presented. It is better to be patient than powerful; it is better to have self-control than to conquer a city (Acts 27:22-25 / Isaiah 56:3, 6).

Some Through The Fire and Some Through The Flood but All Through the Blood.

He allows us go through the storms, the disappointments, tribulation, distress, persecution, and peril, because He trusts that, we will continue to praise Him through the storms, the persecution, the disappointments, the tribulation, the distress, and the danger. When we are in dangerous situations or have difficult decisions to make, and the time comes to decide, you need to have an opinion on the matter.

Here is an example of how the Father would override our decisions: I have been in situations on the highway, and on the roads when God would override my decisions or judgments. Moreover, the Holy Spirit would speak to my spirit and say, "turn this way," "turn that way", "do not move," or "take your time." In addition, every time through His graces, He has kept me from dangerous situations.

I also have heard the testimony of a firefighter, who was in the World Trade Center during the 9/11 attacks. He said that during the time that the trade centers were collapsing, he relied on his training, which he said was very good. But if he would have followed his training, he would have died in the Trade Centers.

However, God the Father, through the Holy Spirit, overrode his decisions to do things what he was trained to do, and began to lead him out of the dangerous situation he was in.

So this is our proof that God the Father takes us in one side and out the other, from beginning to end. All the glory goes to God the Father: So some of us through the fire (which is a purifier), and some of us through the flood (which is washing or being overwhelmed), but all through the Blood (which is atoning or amending).

In order to live, we must plant; and to plant, we must go through the soil, to produce life. The truth is the kernel of wheat planted in the soil. Unless it dies it will be alone-a single seed. However, its death will produce many new kernels-a plentiful harvest of new lives.

Those who love their life in this world will lose it (ref. Matt 16:25). This describes those who serve only themselves. Jesus was going to give the disciples an opportunity to identify this problem in their lives. *"Hates his life"* involves serving Christ. Each believer must establish his or her priorities. We cannot give ourselves fully to this life, and still be committed to the life to come. We must follow Jesus example of self-sacrifice,

Jesus example of "hating" His life in this world so that He could accomplish eternal purposes.

Those who despise their life in this world will keep it for eternity. All those who want to be my disciples must come, and follow me, because my servants must be where I am. Moreover, if they follow me, the Father will honor them. The soil, is the fire, the floods, the storms, the persecutions, the disappointments, and the dangers in our lives. Unless we go through the dirt, we will not be able to reproduce. Therefore, the trials that come, are the dirt in our lives for our survival.

When a seed dies, it produces fruit, and life comes by death. This principle is true not only in nature, but it is also true spiritually. We must purify our hearts, and stop being double-minded, and humble ourselves in the sight of the Lord and He will lift us up (Jas 4:10). Therefore God, who knows the heart, acknowledged them by giving them the Holy Spirit, just as He did to the disciples. He made no distinction between us, and them, purifying their hearts by faith.

Jesus models for the church the kind of love that makes one willing to lay down his life for another, and serve that person even if it means suffering. He loved the church so much that He was willing to suffer, and die for it. His actions not only saved the church, but they also sanctified it. In other words, Jesus wanted to develop the church into what it should be, the holy temple of God.

The phrase *washing of regeneration* refers to the working of the Holy Spirit, who in a moment makes a person new by the cleansing of regeneration (the new birth). This new nature is the ground for living the Christian life, and performing good deeds. The renewing of the Holy Spirit, results in the growth of character and enables the continual process of Christian living and good works.

A complete transformation of the people's ways, lifestyles, and beliefs, was necessary. Thoroughly amend, or "make good" or "do good," normally emphasizes how necessary it is for the transformation of believers and how that takes place. In order for the nation to dwell in the land, it had to be faithful to God.[10]

---

[10] See John 12:24-26; James 4:8-10; Ephesians 5:26-27; Titus 3:5-7 ; Jeremiah 7:3-7

CHAPTER 4

There is Protected
Ground Inside of You!

Protected ground is "the church of the living God, which is the pillar, and the support of the truth." We the church, are the examples, and instructors to the local assemblies, on how we are to function, and we the people of God are the manifested church to the local assemblies around the world. This means that we are to show the people of God, how they are to conduct themselves, and that we will let other future believers know how they must conduct themselves in the household of God.

Therefore, misconduct and disorder in the true church weaken the support of God's truth in the world. Godly men and women gathering in the local assemblies to worship the Lord, which produces an orderly church, testify to others of the truth of God. The peace of God operates in the same way, to protecting the mind from external corrupting influences and to keeping it focused on God's truth (Phil 4:7 NKJV). If you do this, you will experience God's peace, which is far more wonderful than the human mind can understand. His peace will guard your hearts, and minds as you live in Christ Jesus. The peace that Christ gives banishes fear and dread from the hearts of God's children, for Jesus is in control of all circumstances.

Good ground refers to prepared or tilled soil that allows prosperous growth (Matt 13:8 NKJV). However, some seeds fell on fertile soil and produced a crop that was thirty, sixty, and even a hundred times as much as had been planted. Nevertheless, the Lord is faithful; he will make you strong and guard you from the evil One.

"And we confidence in the Lord concerning you, both that you do and will do the things we command you (2 Thes 3: 4 NKJV). The pillar of cloud and fire that protected Israel in its flight from Egypt, actually stood for the Lord himself. Moreover, He says to them that they will leave in a hurry again, running for their lives, because the Lord will go ahead them and protect them from behind.

See also 1Timothy 3:14-15; Philippians 4: 7; 2 Thessalonians 3: 3; Isaiah 52: 12

The Lord Helps His Troubled People

God's has an all-knowing and all-caring interest in His children who serve Him, but He is totally opposite of those who do not follow His path of righteousness. Since not everything in the world functions as it should, even those who do God's will: may undergo suffering for righteousness sake. We have friends who sometimes become our foes because they tell us that no one will help us, not even God. When no one will help us, God is our shield. When we had nothing to treasure, God is our glory. When no one will encourage us, then God Himself would encourage us and lift our heads.

This is possible, only because of God's sustaining power. Given the stress we are faced with it, it is remarkable that we are able to get a night's rest. God's gift of rest given, even in the most troubling times, gives us peace. When God is our protector, there is no need to fear.

Believers should make certain that when they suffer it is only because they have served God faithfully and not because they have done anything wrong. You are blessed! God specially honors those who suffer for doing what is right.

Believers are not encouraged to seek out situations in which they will experience suffering. Instead, believers should make certain that when they suffer it is the result of having been faithful to God rather than because they having done evil.

Suffering may be part of God's perfect and wise plan for a believer. In order to fight the good fight successfully, believers must take on the same mind as Christ. He who has suffered has ceased from sin. Those who serve God faithfully in the midst of suffering take on a different attitude toward sin than what they previously held; sin no longer holds the same grip on them.

Christian should, with the ability which God supplies, rely on His strength. Christians should use the power that God gives them to do His will on earth.

We Are Under Fire

This world has proven to be a hostile environment for the gospel, reminding us that we have become believers "Under Fire." We have to help strengthen our young Christians, with warnings about the suffering they will experience. And we have to take action to establish and encourage the Christians everywhere.

The truth takes root in soil that opposes it; when the "Tempter" cannot prevent the gospel from bringing life to someone, his tactic changes in order to make the young Christians ineffective. Pressures and persecutions are unavoidable. They may come camouflaged; this is his way of causing them not to see clearly the way in which they are to live their lives, what they are to disapprove of, or flat-out experience open hostility. However, in one way or another spiritual growth will always meet resistance. Persecution is demoralizing, but it can also be a cause for taking courage. Without resistance, how can growth be recognized? Trials and tribulations test character; the absence of pressure may indicate a lack of growth. The fellowship that comes from suffering together promotes Christian maturity.

In order for us to encourage our fellow believers who are experiencing extreme persecution at the hands of so-called believers, we must be in favor of holy living. Holy living means behaving ourselves in a sincere manner repeatedly. *Holy* implies sacredness; being consecrated to God or being worthy of God. In order to qualify, a person or thing, has to be free from impurity. There cannot be any hint of moral pollution or spiritual defilement. To be holy is to be free from anything that would offend a perfect God.

This state may seem impossible to achieve; after all, how can imperfect, fallen creatures like ourselves live up to the command to "be holy in all (our) conduct" The answer is found in the opening sentence of Peter's letter. Sanctification; is the process by which we are made holy "of the Spirit" (1 Peter 1: 2 NKJV**).** The Holy Spirit of God, who indwells us through salvation is able to transform us. By the power of the Spirit, we find the ability to "abstain from fleshly lusts, which war against the soul" (2: 11). As we yield ourselves to God and as we soberly and alertly resist the devil (5: 9) and all his temptations, we will find that God is able to "perfect, establish, strengthen, and settle" us (5: 10).

Holy living should be our goal not merely, because God commands it, but because it befits our identity. In Christ, we are no longer citizens of a sinful world, but the "people of God" (2: 10). We are "sojourners and pilgrims" in this world on our way to our true home which is heaven (2: 11). Furthermore, holiness serves an evangelistic purpose; a holy nation is a special people who are able to proclaim praises of Him who called them out of darkness into His marvelous light (2: 9). It's our honorable conduct and "good works" that cause evildoers to glorify God (2: 12).

Finally, Peter speaks of the day when we will stand before God and give an account for the way we have lived. Those who maintained a lifelong fear, referring to the (reverence) of God, will be rewarded for holy living, and they will be best prepared for that day of reckoning (1: 17).

(See also Acts 17:5–9, 13; 1 Thessalonians 2:14–16; 3:42–7 James 1:2–4; 1 Peter 1:15.)

CHAPTER 5

The Lord, The Defender of His People

We must confess God's deliverances and bless the Lord for His deliverances, because He is for us. The enemy desires to swallow us alive (Ps.124:1-8), but God has defeated them all. We are to bless the Lord, for He is the source of our blessing, but we know that we are not always able to keep this balance.

Nevertheless, it is our desire, that balance become a reality in our lives, and at times by God's grace, it does. We are like weaned children: children who are no longer unsettled and discontent, but who are at peace and who trust in their mothers, who are there to comfort them and to meet their needs.

When God's people live together in unity, they experience God's blessings. The blessings of God, flow to His people, and the intent of God, is for the good of His people, both in this life and in the life to come. Even when surrounded by impossible circumstances, believers can proclaim that the Lord is on their side. Moreover, if this so, what can man do to us? If our trust is in the Lord's strength, we do not have to fear the reprisals of our enemies. Although relying on others is a part of living, our ultimate trust is to be placed only in the Lord. Even powerful rulers are limited by their own mortality; though our enemies encircle us, we know that the Lord will help us to triumph over them. They push us to make us fall, but the Lord helps us. Deliverance always come from God; the Lord is not only our Helper, but also our strength and song, and so with our praise of the Lord, and with the goodness and the love of the Most High God, we worship Him.

We must pray that those who rejoice in our misery be proven wrong in their assumption that the Lord is unable to help His people. In this way, the Lord's deliverance will result in God's name being glorified by both the joy of God's people and the shame of His enemies. We must remind ourselves that the Lord is our only source of strength, help, and deliverance. He alone should be praised and worshipped, because if it were not for Him, we would still be at the mercy of our foes. He has given His angels charge over us (Ps. 91); they protect us and help us in our every day life and are there when we need them. Even when our foes think they are defeating us, the promises of our Father are sure.

Our ministry is a ministry of the Spirit, of life, and of righteousness. It is a glorious ministry of liberty, and we do not achieve this by our own human ability, but by God's mercy. We are not weary, tired, or driven to despair, no matter how difficult the task or how great the opposition. We do not retreat in silence but speak boldly because the Spirit motivates us by the grace of God. We are not crushed, or perplexed which means, "to be at a loss." One is perplexed when one sees no way out or in despair, which means "utterly at a loss." As believers, we will face trials, but we must remember that God controls trials and uses them to strengthen His people. God's glory manifests itself through broken vessels to people who endure troubles by relying on His power.

The Lord does not forsake us even though we are struck down, we are not destroyed. The Lord spares our lives so that we can continue to preach the good news and testify to God's deliverances. (See also Psalm 124: 1 – 8; 2 Corinthians 4: 7 – 15).

The Overpowering Love of God

The mastering love of God makes us weak and helpless. It is the very skillful love of God, that lets us know how God cares for us with a true heart and how He leads us with skillful hands. "So he fed them according to the integrity of His heart, and guided them by the skillfulness of His hands." (Ps 78:72 NKJV)

As for us, if we will follow Him with integrity and godliness, always obeying His commands and keeping His laws and regulations, He will establish us. Moreover, may we, His people, always be faithful to the Lord our God. May we always obey His laws and commands, just as we are doing today. Because of the overpowering love of God for us, we are helpless *and* obedient.

Here is an example of the overpowering love of God: When I had turned my back on the church, but not on my faith, God the Father did not give up on me, nor did He fail to help me or bless me during that season in my life. Instead, He was always there and I felt the presence of the Lord, in spite of my backsliding state.

God is always merciful to us in our weakened, disobedient state.

Nevertheless, we should not take this mercy for granted. We must continue to build our lives on the foundation of our most holy faith. In addition, we must continue to pray as the Holy Spirit directs us. We should live in such a way that God's love can bless us as we wait for the eternal life that our Lord Jesus Christ in His mercy is going to give us.

Show mercy to those whose faith is wavering. Rescue others by snatching them from the flames of judgment. There are still others to whom you need to show mercy, but be careful that you are not contaminated by their sins. I will explain this in a little more depth shortly. We must keep ourselves in the love of God. It is clear that we should be both encouraging others and cultivating our love for Christ, for we cannot be separated from His love.

We have certain obligations to other believers. First, we need to show mercy to those in any kind of spiritual or physical need. Second, we need to use discernment in helping our brothers and sisters in the church. Some will require tender care and patience to help them grow in Christ. With others, we may need to use drastic action to rescue them from the temptations of sin.

In rescuing our fellow believers, there is always the need to use wisdom and caution to prevent getting caught up in the sin that caused them to fall, "considering yourself lest you also be tempted."(Gal 6:1 NKJV). For example, a doctor can catch a disease from treating a patient, so one restoring a fallen sinner can be *tempted* to fall into the very sin they are trying to deliver one from (ref. The Nelson Study Bible, NKJV) .We must praise the Lord, who alone can keep us from being deceived. He does not use the word "*falling*", but "*stumbling*" (Jude 24 NKJV). Only a person who is already walking or running can stumble. The overpowering love of God is able to keep us from stumbling. He guards us in this life, despite all the dangers and pitfalls that the deceiver put in our way. Only God can save us, cleanse us from our sins, and present us to Him as faultless, for God is the author and perfecter of our faith (Jude 24 NKJV). Therefore, this is the overpowering love of God, I am talking about; He helps us to live this life, which without Him we would not be able to do. Thank you so very much, Father!

God Is Our Provision

God is our provider and our supplier. "For I know that this will turn out for my deliverances through your prayer and the supply of the Spirit of Jesus Christ" (Phil.1:19, NKJV). Prayer generates the Spirit's supply; this is the channel for His deliverance. The prayer of believers on behalf of other believers is vitally important, because by it, together with the work of the Holy Spirit, God produces positive results. The word "*supply*" here means "to give the abundant resources that would meet one's need." God will provide for all who are apart of His family, those who perform, and all that they need to succeed. He takes care of all our living expenses, and therefore we are looking forward to getting a full supply of Jesus Christ's Spirit.

Just as apostle Paul said, " For I know that this will turn out for my deliverance through your prayer and the supply of the Spirit of Jesus Christ," Phil.1:19 NKHV).

Paul expressed his positive attitude and confidence about how the sovereign God would work out this difficult situation that he would be delivered.

Deliverance is usually translated as "salvation." This word is used, for physical healing, rescue from danger or death, justification, sanctification, and glorification. There are daily provisions to empower us to endure the troubling situations we face and one of those provisions is our fellow man. It is so important that we understand how we need each other to be successful in our Christian walk.

> "From whom the whole body, joined and knitted together by what every joint supplies, according to the effective working by which every part does its share, causes growth of the body for the edifying of itself in love." (Eph. 4:16 NKJV).

This is essential for full growth; there are no insignificant parts in the body. Anything that builds up believers and the church is there for edification. God is our provision; He provides through our relationship with Christ, which is built through the Holy Spirit and the unity of the believers.

CHAPTER 6

We Have to be Sincere!

We should not engage in any pretending, deception, or dishonesty, and we must be truthful and do things in good faith. We must be real and not superficial, or shallow. We must be serious in our thinking and strong in our feelings. We should not be as those who preach just to make money. We should preach God's message with sincerity and with authority.

Moreover, we know that the God who sent us, is watching us, we know this "by pureness, by knowledge, by longsuffering, by kindness, by the Holy Ghost, and by love sincere." (2Cor 6: 6 NKJV). We must pray that our love for one another will overflow more and more, and that we will keep on growing in our knowledge and understanding For I want you to understand what really matters, so that you may live pure and blameless lives until Christ returns, filled with the fruit of our salvation and the good things that are produced in our lives, by Jesus Christ. This will bring much glory and praise to God (ref., Phil 1:10 NKJV).

The purpose of instruction is that all Christians who are filled with the love of God, come to Him with a pure heart, a clear conscience, and sincere faith. Now you can have sincere love for each other as brothers and sisters, because you were cleansed from our sins when we accepted the truth of the Good News. So see to it that you really do love one another intensely with all our hearts. May God's grace be upon all who love our Lord Jesus Christ, with an undying love (Eph 6:24).

God Will Call Out of You, What He Has Provided in You.

God will awaken; He will bring out, He will stir up, and He will excite in you what He has supplied in you. He will call for and send for, that which He has deposited in you. God's will is not so much as God's intention, as it is the desire of God's heart. God has laid out beforehand, His plan for us. This plan was created in God's counsel, which means it was the result of deliberate determination. However, behind the plan and the counsel was not just a master mind, but also a heart of love. That is why I call this book " *The Fruit's of Christ*," because of the heart of God, and that which He has deposited in me. He then call's for what He has deposited, and He "picks me up, raises me, and carries me," to my destiny in Jesus Christ.

Ephesians 1:9-12 says that God's secret plan has been revealed to us; it is a plan centered on Christ, designed long ago according to His good pleasure. Moreover, this is His plan: at the right time, He will bring everything together under the authority of Christ – everything in heaven and on earth. In addition, because of Christ, we have received an inheritance from God, for He chose us from the beginning, and all things happen just as He decided long ago.

God's purpose was that we who were the first to trust in Christ should praise our glorious God. Moreover, when we believed in Christ, He identified us as His own by giving us the Holy Spirit, whom He promised long ago. The Spirit is God's guarantee that He will give us everything He promised and that

He has purchased us to be his own people. This is just one more reason for us to praise our glorious God.

God has revealed His secret plan. As you read what I have written, you will understand what I know about this plan regarding Christ. Moreover, this is the secret plan: we all have an equal share with the Jews in all the riches inherited by God's children. Both groups have believed the Good News, and both are part of the same body and enjoy together the promise of blessings through Christ Jesus, by God's special favor and mighty power.

I have been given the wonderful privilege of serving Him by spreading the good news. This is amazing! Though I did nothing to deserve it, and though I am the least deserving Christian, there is for me this special joy of telling the people about the endless treasures available to them in Christ. I am one of many who explain to everyone the plan that God, the Creator of all things, had kept secret from the beginning. God's purpose was to show his wisdom in all its rich variety to all the rulers and authorities in the heavenly realms. They would see that this happened when Jews and Gentiles were joined together in His church. This was His plan from all eternity and he has now carried it out through Christ Jesus our Lord.

Because of Christ and our faith in Him, we can now come fearlessly into God's presence, assured of his glad welcome. So be careful not to jump to conclusions before the Lord returns as to whether someone is faithful. When the Lord comes, He will bring our deepest secrets to light and will reveal our private motives. Then God will give to everyone whatever praise is due.

"Don't Let Religious Practices Condemn You!"

We must not let those religious leaders, who do not promote love and peace, to draw us into prejudice behavior. In addition, if we become respecters of persons, this makes us partial in ourselves, and we will have become judges of evil thoughts. If we have respect to persons, we commit sin and are guilty of breaking that law. If we favor some people more than others, how then can we claim that we have faith in our glorious Lord Jesus Christ. When men unknowingly boast about their headship in the family, they are being partial in themselves and are becoming judges with evil thoughts. You must not seek favor for yourself, but for others.

Colossians 2: 20 – 23, suggests that religion is a particular system of beliefs or a philosophy of life. In verse 23, Paul mentions *regulations*: Since believers have been released from ritualistic observances, why should they let others bind them down again with these regulations? No human work can add to the merit of Christ's death. His work on the cross is the only acceptable work in God's eyes. The legalistic commands of others are a self-imposed religion, and are of no value for salvation.

James 1: 26 – 27, speaks of the tongue. If we claim to be religious but do not control our tongue, we are just fooling ourselves, and our religion is worthless. Pure and lasting religion in the sight of God our Father means that we must care for orphans and widows in their troubles, and refuse to let the world corrupt us. We are believers; looking into the perfect law of liberty, which is the law of Love. Loving God and loving one's neighbor sums up the Law. However, Christ's love frees us from our sins, and frees us to love others. Orphans and widows were among the most unprotected and needy classes in the ancient societies. Pure religion, does not merely give material goods for the relief of the distressed, it also oversees their care.

In Romans 12: 1 – 2, God entreats believers to present their bodies as a living sacrifice, meaning they should use their bodies to serve and obey Him. Such giving of the body to God is more than a contrast with a dead animal sacrifice; it is "newness of life." *Holy* means set apart for the Lord's use; *acceptable* means pleasing to Him; and *reasonable* indicates that such a gift is the only rational reaction to all the good gifts God has showered on us. So rest in the finished work of Christ and we will not make our spouses, children, brothers and sisters in Christ feel insignificant in this walk of faith.

CHAPTER 7

The Substance Is Of Christ

Christ is genuine and the most important participant in our relationship with the Father. Jesus Christ is the main purpose and is at the center of our Christian faith.

Colossians 2: 6 – 23, teaches not only were our personal sins forgiven, at the cross, but that those rules that condemned us, have also been removed, by the death of Christ. Men especially must be careful not to fall into pride, because the Word of God said says that women are to submit themselves unto their husbands as unto the Lord.

Christ's victory on the cross over the powers that opposed Him and over those that exalted themselves over Him, have been defeated. Anyone who is opposed to His authority and those who are exalting their authority, are acting against Christ's authority in His people lives. They are guilty of evil. This also applies to everyone in authority, including the husbands. This does not mean that a husband is not the head of the wife, and it does not mean that he has the responsibility to see that his wife obeys God's word. That responsibility belongs with the wife and her relationship with her Lord.

Moreover, it does not mean that we are not to submit ourselves unto those in authority. However, it does mean that, we are to submit ourselves unto those in authority as we also do unto Christ's authority. Those that have authority over us do not have the responsibility for our behavior. We should not let these powers and the principalities of the other denominations control us, over which Christ has already triumphed. People will try to bind us up with the outward observances of certain denominations, with their regulations from which Christ has already freed us.

People who do not champion salvation in Christ alone often appear to be humble; but when they are searching for a new spiritual experience, and begin to speak and write in support of some work as being necessary for salvation, it is actually human pride. They do not want to submit to God's plan of salvation revealed in the Bible. We must not let doctrine, traditions, masculinity, or femininity destroy our relationship with our Lord Jesus Christ. Our relationship with Jesus is the most importance substance in our life. To allow pride and the desire to control one another, to ruin our relationships with one another, is selfish and self-centered. Christ is our substance, and nothing else shall take His place.

Cry Out To God And He Will Deliver You!

Call out and shout with much sorrow, cry out in pain loudly! Make a loud sound with your voice, which will arouse God. Shout out with a cry that is much different, with which you can get the attention of the Father, for that which you are pleading and need greatly, and eagerly chase Him with much weeping. These are the attributes, of a person who is of a contrite spirit feeling very sorry for having done wrong.

Psalm 34: 18 – 19, teaches when showing such feeling, God will respond to and inhabit the cries of His people. The Lord is close to the brokenhearted; he rescues those crushed in spirit.

Moreover, when we are walking according to the standard of God, we will face many troubles, but the Lord will rescue us, from every one of them.

Psalm 145: 18 – 19 says, "The Lord is close to all them who call upon Him, yes; to all who call on Him sincerely. He fulfills the desires of those who fear Him; He hears their cries for help and rescues them." Isaiah 57:15 NKJV says "For thus says the High Lofty One, Who inhabits eternity, whose name is Holy:"I dwell in that high and holy *place*, with him *who* has a contrite and humble spirit, to revive the spirit of the humble and to revive the heart of the contrite ones." They may trip seven times, but each time they will rise again. However, one calamity is enough to lay the wicked low. The sacrifice you want is a broken spirit; actions not accompanied by a contrite heart are not acceptable to God. Shall God not avenge His own elect? God will respond to injustice and religious persecution that is dealt out to His people.

In Jonah 2: 1 – 2, Jonah acknowledges that God has helped him and he thanked Him for it. Even though he was disobedient, he was a true believer in God. He "cried for help," his cry came as a scream to God, and because Jonah was terrified, God answered him. So cry out to God with a contrite heart and He will answer!

Pick Me Up, Father, I Do Not Like What I See Down Here.

We sometimes are not pleased with the view of life, from a human standpoint. Therefore, we tend to be discouraged and confused, on which direction in life to take. We see life from our view, which gives us a false sense of reality, rather than the real view of life God has prepared for us.

Matthew 6: 33(NKJV) says, "But seek first the kingdom of God and His righteousness and all these things shall be added to you."

What are "all these things added unto you? Everything we need to sustain life will be added to you", but we must desire righteousness, peace, and the joy of the Holy Spirit. Then we will not have to concern ourselves with our everyday necessities, all we have to do is trust in our Father for all our needs. We then can stretch out our arms to the Father in heaven, saying, "Pick me up Daddy; I don't like what I see down here." He then picks us up, so that we can see things from His perspective.

2 Samuel 22: 51(NKJV) says, *"He* is the tower of salvation to His king, and shows mercy to His anointed, to David and his descendants forevermore." A wide view that is seen, as from a tower, is from God's viewpoint; when we are in that tower, we see a thing from God's perspective. We have every chance of succeeding and getting everything we ask for from the Father.

It is as though we are in a picture, and when we are in the picture, we cannot see the full gamut, that is "the full range of anything." In this case, the picture would be our lives. Moreover, God uses our Lord Jesus Christ as a *gambit* that is "an opening move in *chess* (life) in which a *pawn* (Christ) is risked to get some advantage." This does not mean that our Lord was of less value, because I used the word pawn to describe Him. So let me explain it the following way.

We are in a play, God is the playwright, Christ is the lead actor in this play, and we all have small parts to play. We are just as those who have parts to play in life (Hollywood movie), but we do not have the full story until we read the Bible (script). The whole story revolves around Christ (the lead Actor), who is the main character in the whole play. But God, who knows the beginning and the end of the story, has given us the Bible (script) so that we may know our lines as (character) and the way we are to behave (act).

This is where we are picked up when we do what, 2 Timothy 2: 15(NKJV) says, "Be diligent to present yourself approved to God, a worker who does not need to be ashamed, rightly dividing the word of truth." We must know our lines, in order for us to show ourselves approved unto God, and to do that we must study the Bible.

A good actor learns lines so he will not fail when it is time to shine. So when we say to the Father, "pick me up, I don't like what I see down here." He then lifts us up to His level, so that we can see the whole picture, from His perspective. He is the director, producer, and the author of our faith. He gives us the ability to perform, because He is the "Author" and He wrote the Book. Moreover, He is the "Producer," the One who brings forth and gets us ready for public display. Moreover, He is the "Director," the one who directs or manages the work of His children. We would be astounded at what would happen if we, asked the Lord to pick us up, because we do not like the view, from down here.

CHAPTER 8

The Holy Spirit Will Take Me Where He Has Ordained Me

The Holy Spirit will take me where the Father has arranged for me, and has established for me to go and to do what He has established for me. I am keenly aware that God had determined His call on my life long before my conception. Jeremiah 1: 4 – 19, tells me that, as God's word became a reality in my life, I began to understand that God knew me and had called me to proclaim a critical message at a crucial point in history.

The word *knew* in this passage refers to an intimate knowledge that comes from relationship and personal commitment. That intimate relationship was made apparent in God's sanctifying work, whereby I was "set apart" (made holy) for special service. My role is to be a messenger of God for all people. I would not go and speak alone or of my own accord, but according to the word of the Lord and with God's powerful presence.

The term *deliver* is used to indicate the saving of the people from their captors, the deliverance of the poor from their oppressors, and the safety of the man of God from possible harm before national leaders. *"I am with you"* is God's reassurance to me of His presence and protection. In moments of personal crisis, I prayed these words back to God.

I was commissioned for this task and the essence of my message was outlined. *"I have put my words in your mouth"* means that the source of my message was clearly the Lord, but the message would be expressed through the personality, experience, and artistic ability of the man of God. The message is the Lord's and its expression is accomplished through His servants, the men of God. The people and their leaders will fight against God's servants and His message, but they will not overcome us, because God Himself protects and fights for the faithful.

In 1 Corinthians 2: 1 – 16, Paul teaches that we should not rely on the eloquence of our speech to convince our listeners. Instead, we give the testimony of God, which is revealed by the Holy Spirit. The focal point of my preaching is Jesus Christ. Even though I have many strengths of my own, I wanted to be counted among those who rely on God's strength, rather than using the rhetoric of the day to win converts. I like giving straightforward messages.

The Holy Spirit does not just simply dictate words to us, but He teaches us. The Spirit teaches that the spiritual truths of God are combined with the spiritual vocabulary of the men of God. The natural man or the natural person does not have the Spirit of God, in contrast to the Christian who does have the Spirit. *Receive* in this passage means "to welcome" by "applying" the meaning to life. All we have to do is yield ourselves to the Spirit of God, and He will take us to where (God) has ordained us to be.

When We Worship Nothing Has Changed, but Everything Is Okay!

When we are preparing for church, we may be facing some problems at home such as financial troubles, sickness, Job loss, or bad relationships. Although we are heading for church, we tend to allow our circumstances to hinder our worship of God when we arrive there. We can get this thought into our spirit; it is not how well things are going at home that matters, but how much we worship Him, regardless of the situations. There could be chaos all-around, but our Father responds to our needs the most, as when we are worshiping Him. Regardless of the storms, and the floods of life, we continue believing in Him. We have to, because we are totally and completely trusting in Him regardless of the circumstances we are going thru in our lives.

Exodus 3: 5 – 7, speaks of Moses' encounter with the living God, which set him apart from everything that, is natural. In our own encounter with God, just as with Moses, He lets us know that He knows the misery that we are in; and that He has heard our cries for deliverance out of our harsh situations. He is aware of our suffering.

In Exodus 34: 14, we learn that worship was created by and set up for God alone; we must not worship no other gods, but only the Lord, for He is our God who is passionate about His relationship with us. Davis says in Psalm 29: 2 that, when we worship God, we ascribe to the Lord the glory due to Him, by saying; "worship the Lord in the beauty of holiness." By doing this, we encourage those around us to give honor to the Lord. We can worship, because of Christ's sacrifice on our behalf. Because of the sacrifice that Jesus made for us, we have the words of God inside of our hearts and minds so that we can obey them.

In Hebrews 12: 28 – 29, teaches that we should worship God with reverence. Because we are receiving a kingdom that cannot be destroyed, let us be thankful and please God by worshiping Him with holy fear and awe, for our God is a consuming fire. James tells us that when we draw near to God, he draws near to us, and that we should wash our hands and purify our hearts (4:8). We have to, because true worship is a matter of the heart.

In Jeremiah 17: 21 – 27, the sanctity of the Sabbath was a most serious matter. The Sabbath stood as a sign of creation and the covenant relationship between God and believers. To hallow it is to set it apart, to distinguish it from other days. If the Sabbath were kept holy, this would signify the covenant faithfulness of the believers. If stipulations followed, the temple would once again become the center of worship for the believers. The consequence of disobedience would be total destruction of the city. If stipulations were not followed, the Lord of the covenant would bring an unquenchable, destructive fire against the city and its assemblies.

Gods Extreme Measures to Save Us

God used every means necessary to deliver us from the enemies of sin and death. In John 3: 16 - 18, He proved it by the death of His only begotten Son. The Son of God is the Father's one and only unique Son. Although the Father has begotten many children through the new birth, none of us, are exactly like Jesus Christ, the unique Son of God. His son-ship is from eternity. As the unique Son of God, He has a special glory and the best place of honor.

John teaches that we see God through love. The love of God for His children was visibly demonstrated through Jesus' work on the cross, on our behalf (1John 4:12-16). The only begotten Son expresses the sense of uniqueness. Jesus is the unique Son of God; no other person is God's Son the way He is. Life and judgment are through the Son.

John 5: 24–30 says that, all who believe in the One who sent Christ, will believe in Christ. A judgment to decide a person's eternal destiny is no longer possible for the one who has already been given eternal life. However, all believers will stand before the judgment seat of Christ not for punishment of sin, but to determine inheritance in the Messiah's kingdom. Christ can give life. Because He Himself possesses life, He not only has a part in giving it, He is the source of it. This is another testimony to Jesus' deity, because only God has life in Himself.

Psalm 91: 1- 16, says that there must be a confession of confidence in the Lord. The person who trusts in God is the one who lives close to Him. We can have assurance that those who trust in the Lord need not fear evil, like "perilous pestilence." This is an example of the danger that might come to the believers.

God is compared to a mother hen who gives the believers refuge under His wings when they come to Him. *Shield and buckler* indicates that we have complete protection from all harm, God is an all-protective shield for the believers. Believers in the Lord are protected from any assault, the punishment of the wicked is as sure as the deliverance of the righteous.

The promises of God's protection to the coming One and the coming One's faith in God are the same for the believers. The Father will protect Him no matter what the danger. There is a description of the Lord's protection of the coming One; it has the idea of "holding close to," even "hugging tightly in love" it is an intimate, experiential knowledge of the Father.

CHAPTER 9

Absolute Trust

In Isaiah 30: 15, *quietness and confidence* may be rephrased, as, "utter trust." Trusting in God's strength instead of our own strength is the only way we can find true rest. Instead of trusting in the Lord, the people were depending on the world's system to provide for them and their families. Isaiah denounces those who seek human support, instead of depending on the Lord; they are looking for handouts.

He also addresses the specific folly of depending on the world's system and devising plans independently of God. Shame, which is deep humiliation and not choosing to obey the Lord, comes from rejecting the Lord and despising His message. Returning to God entails repentance, and rest. Trusting in oneself or in this world system serves no useful purpose to us who are His people.

The Lord still waits for you to come to Him, so He can show you His Love and compassion. The Lord; is a faithful God and blessed are those who wait for Him to help them. Only by returning to the Lord and waiting for Him can you and I be saved. However, destruction is certain for those who are rebellious, and who make plans that are contrary to His will. Some weave a web of plans that are not from the Spirit of the Lord, and they therefore pile up their sins. By not consulting God, some have gone down to the world to find help. You have put your trust in the world for its protection, but in trusting the world, you will be humiliated and disgraced. For though they talk of dreams and goals; it will all turn out to their shame, because they will not help you even one little bit the world's promises are worthless.

A time is coming, when we will not able to buy or sell without the mark of the beast. Therefore, absolutely trusting the Lord for all our needs is very important ; we should look to Him for everything. We must practice faith and trust in God, for he cares for us. He tells us not to take any thought for what we shall wear or what we shall eat. There must be total dependency upon the Lord for our survival, which is "absolute trust."

I Shall Not Be, I Shall Not Be Moved

I have known a song for years with the chorus, "I shall not be, I shall not be moved, just like a tree that's planted by the rivers of water." Awakened within my spirit, rooted by a continuous flow of nourishment and because of our roots, I cannot be moved.

Psalms 1: 3 says that, the way of the righteous is like a tree and everything about that tree is valuable and productive. Likewise, the righteous are valuable and productive to God and in whom He finds pleasure. Moreover, they shall prosper, this is not a guarantee of the future financial worth of the righteous; rather, the righteous person is always useful and productive to the Lord. This teaches that one who trusts in God will not be free from trials and adversity, but that God will bring fruit and blessing in and through those difficulties.

We are encouraged and urged to walk in silent confidence in the victory of God over all of our enemies, because through Him salvation was founded. Moreover, it must be declared that we are completely trusting in God. In silent waiting, I can express silent resignation before the sovereign will of the living God. He is my protection and I shall not seriously stir. This is my way of expressing my confidence in God, which is where my strength lies.

The Psalmist wrote in Psalms 62: 2 - 8, that he is strengthened through trusting in God, at all times. By pouring out our hearts before God and by our total dependence on God, we are strengthened. This is why he uses the phrase: *not greatly moved.* God was his refuge; therefore, he could have a calm resolve to wait for the deliverance of God. That is why we shall not be moved either, because we are like trees planted by the rivers of water.

In Jeremiah 17: 5 – 13, one cannot trust in both God and humankind; to turn one's heart toward people is to turn away from God. There are benefits and blessing that accrue to those who have devoted themselves to the Lord and His Word. The heart of Man is the mind, the source of thinking, feeling and action. Any man who unjustly gains wealth will forsake that wealth and then be recognized as a fool.

A fool is a person without moral, ethical, or spiritual character, and as such he cannot expect deliverance and the restoration of the faithful. He has nowhere to turn because they have forsaken God and His lordship, is one and only one source of life and hope for man – the Lord, the fountain of living waters. Though we have struggled with difficulties, including persecution and loneliness, we have continually praised the Lord who, can heal and save. Likewise, the only hope of man's healing and salvation is divine intervention.

CHAPTER 10

The Seed Is The Doorstop That Props Open The Door.

The seed is your doorstop that holds open the door, so that God can bring your promised blessing to you. This is a metaphor similar to a hotel bellhop who is responsible for carrying up your luggage. Because of all the luggage, you have brought with you, he has to pull out his doorstop to prop the door open to get everything inside the room. Likewise, that which you sow into the kingdom of God, is the doorstop that props open the door, so that God can get everything that He has promised to you.

Ecclesiastes 11: 1 – 6, says to give generously, for your gifts will return to you later. Divide your gifts among many, for you do not know what risks might lie ahead. When the clouds are heavy, the rain comes down. When a tree falls, whether south or north there it lies. If you wait for perfect conditions, you will never get anything done. God's ways are as hard to discern as the pathways of the wind and as mysterious as a tiny baby being formed in its mother's womb. Be sure to stay busy and plant a variety of crops for you never know which will grow – perhaps they all will.

I urge you to be generous to as many people as possible – and then some. Regardless of which way a tree falls, someone is going to get the use of its wood, so stop worrying that it did not fall on your side of the fence, (or even hoping that it will). The person who is so cautious, that he must wait for the ideal time, before he makes a move is doomed to fail. Some works of God defy explanation. Moreover, God who made everything and who is the Creator, is not limited to the inability of humans to know God's works apart from knowing Him. Do not hold back from getting involved. Let the success or failure of a task rest in the hand of God – but get to the task.

Our Seed Is the Protector for Our Blessing

1 Kings 17: 8 – 24, tells the story of the man of God talking to the widow; "But put together for me a small cake from it first." The challenge to the widow would call for faith, in the midst of her desperate circumstances. This also points the widow directly to Him who is the sustainer of all. God supplied the daily necessities to a non – Israelite who willingly took Him at His word. The fresh supply of oil and flour each day would be a reminder to both the prophet and the widow of the value of personal trust in Him, who alone is sufficient to meet every need. She always had plenty of flour and oil left in the containers until the time when the Lord send rain and the crops could grow again!

Therefore, she, Elijah, and her son continued to eat from her supply of flour and oil for many days. No matter how much consumption there was always enough in the containers, just as the Lord had promised through Elijah. The widow-sowed seed into the prophet's life, therefore the promise of her harvest or blessings was sealed. In addition, her obedience to the word of the man of God, protected her blessing and her family.

Let No Man Take Your Crown!

Revelation 3: 11, speaks of our crown. Through misconduct, we can lose our crown that we had previously attained. A crown is a symbol of honor that goes to the one who is victorious.

In 2 John 8, the disciple warns his readers: "Watch out, so that you do not lose the prize for which you have worked so hard. Be careful, so that, you will receive your full reward." If an athlete wins a contest, but is later, found with drugs in his or her system, she could be stripped of her prize. The crown of Life goes to the believer, who perseveres under trials. Such perseverance will result in the ultimate enjoyment of life in God's kingdom.

Do not let people take your crown, through unforgiveness, because Jesus said; "If you forgive not, He will not forgive you (Mk 11:26, Matt 6:15; 18; 35)." I remember a story of a man, who died and the angels came, and took him, to both heaven, and hell. However, when he was shown hell he was told, that he would have taken his part in the lake of fire, if he had not, the Father.

What had happened before he died, was that he had an argument with his wife. She hit him, but knowing she was wrong for hitting her husband, she then begged him for forgiveness but he refused to forgive her. He left home, and died in a car accident. The angel of God came and took him to heaven, and showed him heaven and hell. He explained to him, that because he had refused to forgive his wife, that he was headed to hell. The angel was there to remind him, that if he did not forgive, that God would not forgive him.

Matthew 6:14-15 suggests that, if you do not forgive, neither will your Father in heaven forgive your trespasses. Therefore, misconduct can cause you to lose your crown or reward.

Attacking the Work of God

"And now I say to you, keep away from these men, let them alone: for if this plan or this work is of men, it will come to nothing; But if it is of God, you cannot overthrow it; lest you even be found, to fight against God" (Acts 5:38-39, NKJV). When you are attacking the men of God, you are attacking God. Therefore, my advice is, leave these men alone. If they are teaching and doing these things merely on their own, it will soon be overthrown. However, if it is of God, you will not be able to stop them. You may even find yourselves fighting against God. These are the kinds of people who are always, tearing down what they believe is wrong with others and they ever build up. The Damascus Experience, the response of believers to the gospel was like kicking against a sharp point.

When people live as children of God, they do what is right, because they are righteous, even as Christ is righteous. The one who does not obey God's commands and does not love other Christians, belong to God.

The foundation is built, and now others are building on it. But, whoever is building on this foundation must be very careful. In addition, each builders work will be tested by fire, to see if it keeps its value. God's temple is holy, and Christians are that temple.

Now all of us together are Christ's body, and each one of us is a separate and necessary part of it.

As God's partners, I beg you not to reject this marvelous message of God's great kindness. We try to live in such a way, that no one will be hindered from finding the Lord, by the way we are acting, and so that no one will find fault with our ministry. In everything, we do, we try to show that we are true ministers of God. We patiently endure troubles, hardships, and calamities of every kind. We have been beaten, put in jail, faced angry mobs, worked to exhaustion, endured sleepless nights, and have gone without food. We have proved ourselves by our purity, our understanding, our patience, our kindness, our sincere love and by the power of the Holy Spirit. We have faithfully preached the truth; God's power has been working in us.

We have righteousness as our weapon, both to attack God's opponents and to defend ourselves. We serve God whether people honor us or despise us, whether they slander us or praise us. We are honest, but they call us impostor. We are well known, but treated as unknown. We live close to death, but here we are, still alive. We were beaten within an inch of our lives, our hearts ached, but we always had joy. We are poor, but we give spiritual riches to others. We own nothing and yet we have everything.

If there is a problem between us, it is not because of a lack of love on His part, but because we have withheld our love from Him. I am talking now as I would to my own children. I tell them to open their hearts to us! Moreover, I let them know that I am learning how to be a parent. In other words, we are not parents by trade, just as we are not carpenters by trade. To be able to build a structure takes skills. However, to destroy a structure, does not take any skills at all.

(See also Acts 5:38-39; 1Corinthians 3:9-17; 12:27; 2 Corinthians 6:1-13)

CHAPTER 11

Sailing in a Stormy Season

God's people are advised not to sail in dangerous seasons. Nevertheless, the warnings are rejected, because greed and the desire for comfort has gotten in the way of good sense. Just as the helmsman and the owners of the ships were able to persuade the centurion to sail regardless of the warnings of Paul, this is exactly the way it is in the church today. Who is persuading members of the body of Christ, to reject the counsel of the men of God?

Yet in Acts 27:14, not long after a dangerous storm had arisen there were those, who were hurt and suffered much damage to the structure of their ship and to their lives. In verses 18-25, Paul said, to the men on the ship that they should have listened to him in the first place and not left Fair Havens. Moreover, they would have avoided all this injury and loss. However, he tells them to take courage! None of them will lose their lives, even though the ship will go down. The all-powerful and all-knowing God had said; that no one would be lost who remained on the ship. He had given Paul absolute assurance. Yet in verse 31, Paul warned that unless the sailors stayed with the ship, the Roman soldiers would lose their lives, also. Moreover, because they listened; to Paul's warning, they stopped the sailors from leaving the ship and everyone made it ashore alive. We can make it also, if we will obey the Word of God, which comes out of the mouth of the men of God. Moreover, we can avoid a "shipwreck," and everyone will make it to the shore alive.

God fulfilled His purpose and promise through the warnings of Paul and the choices of the soldiers. Likewise, God will fulfill His purpose and promise through the warnings of those who are the leaders in your church and through the choices of the members of your church. Yet in verse 40, they let go the anchors and left them in the sea, loosed the rudder ropes, and they raised the mainsail to the wind and made for shore.

Hebrews 12: 1(NKJV) says, "Therefore we also, since we are surrounded by so greater cloud of witnesses, let us lay aside every weight, and the sin which so easily ensnares us, and let us run with endurance the race that is set before us."

Because they sailed doing the stormy season, their ship was destroyed, and Paul told the others to try for it on planks and debris from the broken ship. Therefore, everyone escaped safely ashore! Because we too, fail to listen to leadership, we therefore have planks and debris from our broken lives to make it to shore. (see also Acts 27: 9 – 11 NKJV)

A Zeal for God

There are those who have enthusiasm for God, but it is aimed at the wrong thing. Outwardly, they are very religious. However, they did not make their effort according to knowledge. They lacked a correct understanding of the kind of worship God wanted from them. Moreover, when they did come to an understanding of the true knowledge of God, they understood the righteousness God gives, through the person of Jesus Christ. They did not obey God's command to believe, in Christ, through whom all the requirements of the Law have been fulfilled. Moreover, Christ was the object to which the law led. The point is that they are ignorant of God's righteousness, because they failed to comprehend what the Law's true intentions was. The law revealed sin and showed that people could not hope to keep the law. Christ came and fulfilled it, then offered us His righteousness through faith in Him.

There are two kinds of righteousness, by works or by faith. One is inaccessible, and the other is very accessible. Righteousness by faith is not far off and inaccessible, but it is as near as a person's mouth and heart. All one has to do is repent, believe in Jesus, and confess that belief. One has to confess with the mouth, for salvation (Rom 10:5-11).

One of the conditions for salvation is righteousness, which is justified, and this comes from an internal faith. Another condition of salvation, which means deliverance from wrath and from the power of sin, is external confession, which is calling on the Lord for help. Why have some people not attained it? The answer is that they did not obtain righteousness because they did not believe. They tried obtaining righteousness by the works of the law. Being zealous to righteousness by works, they stumbled over the righteousness of faith offered in Christ.

This is my fear for the church as well, just as Paul was concerned for the Galatians, when he wrote to them. When I gave my life to the Lord, that was the most liberating feeling I had ever felt. I was raised in a Baptist church, but my liberty was challenged, and I was very uncomfortable in my surroundings. Therefore, I exercised my liberty in Christ, which they took it as a threat to the leadership of the church. As a result, I received a lot of religious verbal abuse. My brother and I were told often to watch what we were saying; they felt as though we were trying to take over the church. Because the Lord was using us to share the truth of the gospel and not the traditions of the Baptists denomination, they were happy that we left.

This leads me to my point concerning my fears for the church. "Is it spiritual progress to be enslaved again to things that are weak and worthless rituals and observances? How could you have known God and turned away to 'childish' things?" (See also 1 Cor. 13:11; Gal 4:3; 9-11)

The Galatians had come to know God through faith in Jesus Christ. He had adopted them as His own sons, but they were turning back to the law that had once enslaved them.

I urge you, to get beyond the ceremonial rules and regulations, preach the gospel of Christ, and stop hindering the gospel of Christ with laws and regulations. A person with pure motives and real friendship does not always say things that are pleasant to hear. My brother and I were telling the congregation the truth, and as a result, we were labeled as their enemy. Sometimes the truth hurts, but a faithful friend would courageously confront another.

Paul's own career of persecuting Christians proved that zealous behavior could be tragically misguided. His zeal for the Law was blinding him to the freedom and the truth found, in Jesus Christ. Understanding such realities, the believer in Christ must continue steadfastly in the liberty of not having to keep the Law of Moses in order to live.

Faith in Christ brings about not only justification before God, but also growth in the Christian life until we are completely glorified by God and freed from the presence of sin. This is the hope of righteousness; of which we are assured. We will be righteous before the Lord on that last day, because we have a foretaste of that righteousness from the Spirit who lives within us. 15(See also Romans 10:1-4; Galatians 4:8-20.)

CHAPTER 12

Hidden in the Lord

The people who were doomed for judgment or destruction in the day of the Lord were commanded to gather, perhaps in repentance. "Seek the Lord;" (Acts 17:27, 28 NKJV), this is the language of true repentance, renewal, and regeneration. We will be hidden even in the midst of the most dangerous of scenes. The mercy and grace of the Lord, is still available to a repentant people. In order for us to be "hidden in the Lord," (Zeph 2:1-3), we must first return to Him and call upon His name. Then we will be hidden in the Lord, "protected" from the pending judgment or destruction that is coming upon the nations.

We are to seek God's standard of living, which is righteousness, meekness, humility, right living, and justice. Perhaps; even yet the Lord will protect you from His anger on that day of destruction, when God will arise in judgment to save all the meek of the earth. This is where being hidden in the Lord pays off, even though we are still doing things our way and walking according to our own desires. We are going on unprotected, not under the shadow of the protective wings of our Lord. "For who has resisted His will?" (Rom 9:19 NKJV)

Prayer must become propriety, because God said; "those who have turned back from following the Lord, and have not sought the Lord, nor inquired of Him"(Zeph. 1:6). The same destruction, that will come upon the wicked, will also fall upon them. Amos pleaded with Israel to return to God and avoid the judgment He otherwise would bring upon them. When we are obedient to the call of God, which is a form of worship and it will invoke the Lord's presence with us in our spoken prayers and blessings.

If we began to live as God has taught us in the Law, He would indeed be with us. A visit from God is a dreaded and mournful event for anyone not ready to meet Him. The bible speaks of Jesus Christ, as "Hidden Manna" (Rev 2:17) to eat, that person who overcomes by faith amidst terrible circumstances will receive "hidden manna" to eat. Hidden manna is a reward for faithfulness to God, and suggests special intimacy with Christ.

Over-comers are promised supernatural provisions in the resurrected state, to enable them to function effectively as co-rulers in Christ's kingdom. He who overcomes is one who keeps God's words until the end. To this faithful believer, Christ promises the privilege of ruling and reigning with Him, in His kingdom and sharing in His royal splendor. Only those believers who are over-comers and who persevere in obedience to the end of life have the promise of being co-heirs with Christ. He will share His sovereignty with messianic partners who have proven their trustworthiness in this life by doing the will of God to the end. All believers should desire to achieve this exalted destiny. 16 (See also Psalm 76:9; Amos 5:6, 14–15; Zephaniah 1:6, 2:1–3; Romans 9:19; Revelation 2:17.)

Be Whatever Nature You are Hereafter

"He who is unjust, let him be unjust still; he who is filthy, let him be filthy still; he who is righteous, let him be righteous still; he who is holy, let him be holy still" (Rev 22:11). This verse seems to be a prediction that believers and unbelievers will live out their lives true to their nature until the final judgment. The rewarding of each believer according to his or her works is taught in Revelation 22.

Christ's rewards are meant to provide a powerful incentive for an obedient life. We must rigorously discipline ourselves, so as not to disqualify ourselves from the reward of reigning with Christ. The judgment seat of Christ can be a time of great regret, or it can be an occasion of supreme joy.

After Christ comes again, he will give rewards to His own, because He is in control of all history and eternity. *Blessed*, (Rev 22:14) suggests a quality of life involving an intimate fellowship with Jesus Christ based upon a persevering obedience. This may fulfill Christ's provision of life and life that is more abundant. No one can enter into the city unless his name is written in the Lamb's Book of Life. This beatitude is speaking of those justified by faith, who express that faith is obedience.

The obedient over-comer is promised the reward of entering through the gates of the city, possibly a privilege reserved for those who share in the Lord's victory procession. The desire to be with Christ produces the ambition to please Him. We strive to please the Lord not only because we know we will be with Him, but also because, He will evaluate our work whether good or bad and reward us accordingly.

The person unconcerned about doing good deeds shows a grave lack of vision. For we all must appear, meaning "to make visible" or "to make known," or it could mean believers will stand before the Lord with their true character revealed. *That each one may receive,* means, "To receive back," or "to get one's due." The believer will be either approved or ashamed. This truth should dramatically change the way we live, for our Master will evaluate our actions.

Therefore, indicates that this verse is a conclusion drawn from the previous one. The *terror of the Lord* is the fear of standing before the Lord and having one's life exposed and evaluated. The reality of giving an account to the Lord motivated

Paul to persuade people, in this context, which means to convince the Corinthians of his sincerity and integrity (2 Cor 5:11).

Therefore, I too would like to persuade people to change their ways before it is too late. Because the Lord has stated "the time is at hand," meaning "now," this is the time to change if you are going to change. If you are unjust, you will be unjust hereafter, if you are filthy, you will be filthy hereafter, if you are righteous, you will be righteous hereafter, and if you are Holy, you will be Holy hereafter. 17(See also Revelation 22:11-14; 2 Cor. 5:9-11)

I would like to thank the Lord Jesus Christ for the inspiration for this book. My wonderful wife whom I love dearly.

Minister Tommy & Angela Morris
Pastor & Founders of
The Fruits of Christ Ministries

www.ingramcontent.com/pod-product-compliance
Lightning Source LLC
Chambersburg PA
CBHW020019050426
42450CB00005B/546